Primary Sources in U.S. History

# The JAZZ AGE
## AND THE GREAT DEPRESSION

**ENZO GEORGE**

Cavendish
Square

New York

Published in 2016 by Cavendish Square Publishing, LLC
243 5th Avenue, Suite 136, New York, NY 10016

© 2016 Brown Bear Books Ltd

First Edition

Website: cavendishsq.com

This publication represents the opinions and views of the author based on his or her personal experiences, knowledge, and research. The information in this book serves as a general guide only. the author and publisher have used their best efforts in preparing this book and disclaim liability rising directly or indirectly from the use and application of this book.

CPSIA Compliance Information: Batch #WS15CSQ

All websites were available and accurate when this book was sent to press.

Library of Congress Cataloging-in-Publication Data

George, Enzo.
The Jazz Age and the Great Depression / by Enzo George.
   p. cm. — (Primary sources in U.S. history)
Includes index.
ISBN 978-1-50260-490-3 (hardcover) ISBN 978-1-50260-491-0 (ebook)
1. New Deal, 1933-1939 — Juvenile literature. 2. Depressions — 1929 — United States — Juvenile literature. 3. United States — Economic conditions — 1918-1945 — Juvenile literature. 4. United States — Social conditions — 1933 - 1945 — Juvenile literature. I. George, Enzo. II. Title.

E806.G47 2016
973.916—d23

For Brown Bear Books Ltd:
Editorial Director: Lindsey Lowe
Managing Editor: Tim Cooke
Children's Publisher: Anne O'Daly
Design Manager: Keith Davis
Designer: Lynne Lennon
Picture Manager: Sophie Mortimer

Picture Credits:
Front Cover : All © Library of Congress
All images © Library of Congress, except; 23, © Robert Hunt Library

Brown Bear Books has made every attempt to contact the copyright holder.
If you have any information please contact licensing@brownbearbooks.co.uk

We believe the extracts included in this book to be material in the public domain.
Anyone having further information should contact licensing@brownbearbooks.co.uk

Manufactured in the United States of America

# CONTENTS

# INTRODUCTION

**Primary sources are the best way to get close to people from the past. They include the things people wrote in diaries, letters, or books; the paintings, drawings, maps, or cartoons they created; and even the buildings they constructed, the clothes they wore, or the possessions they owned. Such sources often reveal a lot about how people saw themselves and how they thought about their world.**

A range of primary sources from the 1920s and 1930s, two decades that were times of dramatically contrasting fortunes for Americans, are collected in this book. The period profoundly influenced how they saw their country and their futures.

The 1920s began in the shadow of World War I (1914–1918). Americans shocked by the horrors of the war turned away from the rest of the world. As prosperity rose at home, automobiles and radios became widespread and new influences such as jazz music swept the country. For many people, however, the prosperity turned out to be an illusion. In 1929 the stock market crashed, devastating the economy. A slowdown in trade led to the Great Depression, when millions of Americans lost their jobs. For much of the 1930s the government tried to kick-start the economy while Americans moved around the country in a desperate search for work.

# HOW TO USE THIS BOOK

Each spread contains at least one primary source. Look out for "Source Explored" boxes that explain images from the 1920s and 1930s and who made them and why. There are also "As They Saw It" boxes that contain quotes from people of the period.

Some boxes contain more detailed information about a particular aspect of a subject. The subjects are arranged in roughly chronological order. They focus on key events or people. There is a full timeline of the period at the back of the book.

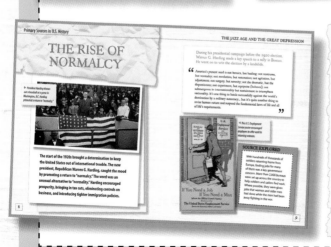

Some spreads feature a longer extract from a contemporary eyewitness. Look for the colored introduction that explains who the writer is and the origin of his or her account. These accounts are often accompanied by a related visual primary source.

# ISOLATIONISM

World War I was more costly in terms of lives than most Americans had expected. By 1918, around 114,000 Americans had in Europe. After the war and a deadly Spanish flu pandemic, many Americans wanted to turn their backs on the world. They wanted to concentrate on U.S. issues, not get caught up in international affairs. This attitude toward the rest of the world was known as Isolationism.

▼ *The "Unknown Soldier" was buried in Washington, D.C., in 1921. The huge losses of the war convinced many Americans to turn their backs on the world.*

## SOURCE EXPLORED

This cartoon was published in *Punch* magazine in London on December 10, 1919. It shows Uncle Sam beside the League of Nations bridge, resting on the keystone that would hold the bridge up. Without U.S. involvement, the cartoon implies, the bridge will collapse. The cartoon is a comment on the fact that the League of Nations was proposed by U.S. President Woodrow Wilson as an organization for settling international disputes. Most Americans did not want to join, however, for fear of being dragged into another war. In March 1920, the U.S. Congress refused to join the League or ratify the Treaty of Versailles that had ended the war.

## AS THEY SAW IT

" We are met to-day to pay the impersonal tribute. The name of him whose body lies before us took flight with his imperishable soul. We know not whence he came, but only that his death marks him with the everlasting glory of an American dying for his country. "

—President Warren G. Harding at the dedication of the tomb of The Unknown Soldier, Arlington Cemetery, November 11, 1921

THIS LEAGUE OF NATIONS BRIDGE WAS DESIGNED BY THE PRESIDENT OF THE U·S·A·

KEYSTONE USA

BELGIUM FRANCE   ENGLAND ITALY

◀ *This* Punch *cartoon reflected a common belief that without U.S. support the League of Nations was bound to fail.*

# THE RISE OF NORMALCY

▶ President Harding throws out a baseball at a game in Washington, D.C. Harding promoted a return to "normalcy."

The start of the 1920s brought a determination to keep the United States out of international trouble. The new president, Republican Warren G. Harding, caught the mood by promoting a return to "normalcy." The word was an unusual alternative to "normality." Harding encouraged prosperity, bringing in tax cuts, eliminating controls on business, and introducing tighter immigration policies.

During his presidential campaign before the 1920 election, Warren G. Harding made a key speech to a rally in Boston. He went on to win the election by a landslide.

" America's present need is not heroics, but healing; not nostrums, but normalcy; not revolution, but restoration; not agitation, but adjustment; not surgery, but serenity; not the dramatic, but the dispassionate; not experiment, but equipoise [balance]; not submergence in internationality but sustainment in triumphant nationality. It's one thing to battle successfully against the world's domination by a military autocracy ... but it's quite another thing to revise human nature and suspend the fundamental laws of life and all of life's requirements. "

◄ This U.S. Employment Service poster encouraged employers to offer work to returning veterans.

## SOURCE EXPLORED

With hundreds of thousands of soldiers returning home from Europe, finding jobs for many of them was a key government concern. More than two thousand bureaus were set up across the country to help soldiers and sailors find work. Where possible, they were given jobs that women and older men had done while the men had been away fighting in the war.

# ECONOMIC BOOM

▲ *Growing numbers of tall blocks—mainly hotels—rise above midtown Manhattan in this photograph from 1923.*

Only a few years after the end of World War I in 1918, America was booming. The economy was growing by 6 percent a year, and industrial output was higher than that of the great powers of Europe combined. U.S. families increasingly owned automobiles, telephones, and radios. By 1927, two-thirds of all homes had electricity. In the optimistic atmosphere, construction boomed. New York City was home to the world's tallest buildings: the Chrysler Building from May 1930 and then the Empire State Building in 1931.

◀ Dozens of Model T Fords await delivery in the Ford Motor Company plant. Thanks to Ford's assembly line, each car took only ninety-three minutes to make.

## SOURCE EXPLORED

This photograph shows rows of completed automobiles in the Ford Motor Company plant in Detroit, Michigan, in around 1925. By the end of the decade, there were more than twenty-six million automobiles on American roads. Henry Ford had developed the assembly line to manufacture the popular Model T, producing fifteen million between 1908 and 1927. Such advances and a fall in the price of rubber for tires brought cars within the budget of families. Taking to the road became easier as the highway network doubled in length, linking together the forty-eight continental states.

## AS THEY SAW IT

❝ We in America today are nearer to the final triumph over poverty than ever before in the history of any land. The poorhouse is vanishing from among us. We have not yet reached the goal, but ... we shall soon with the help of God be in sight of the day when poverty will be banished from this nation. ❞

—Herbert Hoover, accepting the Republican nomination as presidential candidate in 1928

# PROHIBITION

The Eighteenth Amendment came into effect on January 16, 1920. Passed in 1918, the National Prohibition Act banned the sale of liquor in an attempt to end social ills blamed drink. Instead, the alcohol trade became a gold mine for criminals who made vast fortunes (Al Capone was the most notorious of them). People continued to drink—drinking liquor was not itself illegal, just the making and selling of it—at speakeasies, saloons that sold illegal liquor in secret.

▼ New Yorkers crowd a bar for a last drink before a temporary Prohibition measure comes into effect in the city in June 1919.

## SOURCE EXPLORED

New York's Deputy Police Commissioner, John A. Leach (right), watches federal agents pour liquor into a sewer after a raid on an illegal brewery. The Bureau of Prohibition was set up to stop the selling and consumption of alcohol. Prohibition agents were poorly paid, however, and many took bribes from gangsters to ignore their activities. The most famous agent was Eliot Ness, who helped bring down Chicago gangster Al Capone. Two New York City agents, Izzy and Moe (Isidor Einstein and Moe Smith), made 4,932 arrests and confiscated more than five million bottles of alcohol.

## AS THEY SAW IT

" It was during Prohibition. Between sets, we'd sneak into a speakeasy for a drink. One night, we couldn't get in the speak. Jeez, the police were out. Some gangsters killed about three guys. They were pretty top-flight guys, so that was the end of that speakeasy. "

—Jimmy McPartland, cornet player, recalls performing in a speakeasy

◄ Federal agents dispose of liquor after a raid on an illegal distillery in New York City in 1921.

# NEW ROLES FOR WOMEN

▶ *A woman uses a sorting machine in an office in 1921. During the 1920s increasing numbers of women worked outside the home.*

During the war, women worked in factories, offices, and farms in the place of men who were away fighting. Women's contributions to the war effort added weight to their campaign for suffrage, or the right to vote. Decades of campaigning led to the passing of the Nineteenth Amendment. Ratified on August 18, 1920, the amendment gave thirty million women the right to vote. Meanwhile, the changing status of women was reflected in the appearance of the confident young "Flapper."

## SOURCE EXPLORED

This illustration by Russell Patterson is titled "Where there's smoke there's fire." It shows a stylish Flapper smoking. This was seen as outrageous behavior for women in the 1920s, as were the Flappers' habits of drinking alcohol and wearing makeup. Flappers cut their hair short, wore short skirts that "flapped," and listened to jazz. Everything they did broke traditional restrictions on women's behavior.

▲ Russell Patterson's drawings of "Jazz Age" women featured in many popular magazines.

Zelda Sayre Fitzgerald was sometimes seen as the original Flapper. Like her husband, the author F. Scott Fitzgerald, she chronicled life during the Jazz Age. She wrote "Eulogy on the Flapper" for *Metropolitan Magazine* in June 1922.

> " I am assuming that the Flapper will live by her accomplishments and not by her Flapping. How can a girl say again, 'I do not want to be respectable because respectable girls are not attractive' ... Perceiving these things, the Flapper awoke from her lethargy of sub-deb-ism, bobbed her hair, put on her choicest pair of earrings and a great deal of audacity and rouge, and went into the battle ... She was conscious that the things that she did were the things she had always wanted to do ... "

# AMERICAN HEROES

From Henry Ford, who revolutionized the auto industry, to Hollywood movie stars, a group of men—and a few women—came to epitomize the age. Sportsmen such as Johnny Weissmuller, the Olympic swimmer who later became a movie star, were also admired for their achievements. In 1927 tennis player Helen Newington Wills became the first U.S. woman to win the Wimbledon championship in England.

▼ *Babe Ruth (right) shakes hands with President Warren G. Harding in Yankee Stadium shortly after it opened in April 1923.*

▼ *Charles Lindbergh poses next to the* Spirit of St. Louis *on May 31, 1927.*

## BABE RUTH

George Herman "Babe" Ruth was one of the most successful baseball players of all time. A left-handed pitcher and slugger, Ruth played for the Boston Red Sox and later led the New York Yankees to seven World Series titles. The record of sixty homeruns he set in 1927 was not broken until 1961, and he remains first in all-time slugging percentages and all-time on-base-plus-slugging. With Ruth, the Yankees set new records for crowds. When the team built a new stadium in the South Bronx in 1923, it was known as "The House that Ruth Built."

## SOURCE EXPLORED

Charles A. Lindbergh stands next to his airplane, the *Spirit of St. Louis*, after achieving a feat that made him famous around the world. On May 20, 1927, Lindbergh, an experienced aviator and a reserve officer in the U.S. Army Air Corps, took off from Roosevelt Field near New York City to attempt to become the first man to fly nonstop across the Atlantic Ocean. It was a courageous feat. Just two days before his departure, two Frenchmen had set off from Paris for New York but disappeared somewhere over the ocean. Charles Lindbergh flew for 33.5 hours, overcoming lack of sleep, fog, snow, and ice, before successfully arriving in Paris on May 21. He was awarded the nation's highest military award, the Medal of Honor, for his achievement.

# THE JAZZ AGE

The popularity of a new form of music—jazz—gave the Roaring Twenties an enduring nickname, "The Jazz Age." Jazz began in New Orleans in 1915 before moving to Chicago and New York. A mixture of European and African rhythms, jazz captured the mood of freedom that swept America after World War I. In urban centers, the Jazz Age was a time of skyscrapers, clubs, Flappers, and consumerism.

▼ Four young women wait to take part in a beauty pageant in Atlantic City in September 1922.

## AS THEY SAW IT

" The bar is in full swing, and floating rounds of cocktails permeate the garden outside, until the air is alive with chatter and laughter, and casual innuendo and introductions forgotten on the spot, and enthusiastic meetings between women who never knew each other's names. "

–F. Scott Fitzgerald,
*The Great Gatsby,* 1925

◀ *British artist Anne Harriet Fish drew* Dancing Couples *no. 2 in 1921 to show the new relations between the sexes.*

## SOURCE EXPLORED

This illustration drawing for *Vanity Fair* magazine in March 1921 captures the excitement of the Jazz Age. Men and women dance together in a nightclub. Gone are the corsets and petticoats of the prewar era, and the women wear the fashionable clothes of the day: short dresses with revealing backs. Their hair is cut short, some in the helmet-like bob that was popular at the time. The drawing captures the new equality that existed between men and women in the twenties. Women now had the vote and they dressed and behaved as they wanted and not as society traditionally expected them to. The luxurious surrounding of the nightclub shows the kind of clubs well-off city dwellers liked to attend.

# AFRICAN AMERICANS

After 1916 the Great Migration began as African Americans from the South began to move north in search of work. During the 1920s, more than one million African American migrants settled in cities such as Detroit, Chicago, and New York. Harlem, in New York, was the center of a black cultural flowering known as the Harlem Renaissance. Meanwhile leaders such as Marcus Garvey and W.E.B. Du Bois claimed increasing status for African Americans in U.S. society.

▶ Marcus Garvey founded the Universal Negro Improvement Association to try to improve conditions for African Americans.

◀ Men forming a giant "K" lead the Ku Klux Klan march down Pennsylvania Avenue in Washington, D.C.

## SOURCE EXPLORED

In 1926, forty thousand members of the Ku Klux Klan (KKK) marched through Washington, D.C. The march was a reminder of the racism that existed throughout the United States. The KKK (established in 1866) revived during the 1920s, and now targeted not just African Americans but also other foreigners, Jews, and Catholics.

The journalist and minister Rollin Lynde Hartt describes a visit to Harlem in April 1921 in an account published in *The Independent*:

❝ Greatest negro city in the world, it boasts magnificent negro churches, luxurious negro apartment houses, vast negro wealth, and a negro population of 130,000, or possibly 150,000, or, as enthusiasts declare, 195,000. Only fifteen years ago Harlem was white. Today it is an exhibit, not of darkest, but of brightest Africa. No matter what his attitude toward Garvey and Garveyism, every new negro argues, consciously or unconsciously, 'If my race could make Harlem, pray, what on earth can't it do?' ... ❞

# THE RISE OF HOLLYWOOD

The 1920s was the decade of the movies. Americans had been going to movie houses to watch silent films since 1910, but most were newsreels. By the 1920s, movies were being made for entertainment and the film industry based in Hollywood, Los Angeles, was the fourth-largest business in America.

Performers such as Mary Pickford, Lillian Gish, and Rudolph Valentino were huge stars. Even small towns had a movie house; in 1921, there were 15,500 movie theaters across the nation.

◀ This portrait from 1922 shows the movie star Lillian Gish in a gown that captures the glamor of Hollywood.

## SOURCE EXPLORED

This poster from Warner Brothers for the 1927 movie *The Jazz Singer* shows a son serenading his mother. *The Jazz Singer* changed moviegoing forever, because it was the first "talkie." Silent movies had been accompanied by live music, but for *The Jazz Singer* a soundtrack was recorded on a phonograph record and played simultaneously with the movie. The movie marked the end of the era of silent movies. The movie was also notable because its white star, Al Jolson, wore black makeup—something that was more acceptable at the time than it would be today.

WARNER BROS. SUPREME TRIUMPH

AL JOLSON

IN

"THE JAZZ SINGER"

WITH

MAY McAVOY
WARNER OLAND
Cantor Rosenblatt

Based upon the play by Samson Raphaelson as produced on the spoken stage by Lewis & Gordon...Sam H. Harris

Scenario by Al Cohn

DIRECTED BY ALAN CROSLAND

▲ *The Warner Brothers' poster calls the movie a "supreme triumph"—and audiences seemed to agree.*

## THE MOVIE DECADE

The 1920s saw the movies take a central part in U.S. life. Receipts from movie theaters were $750 million in 1921, and reached over $1 billion in 1927. Even early in the decade, around fifty million Americans—half the population— regularly went to the movies. By the end of the decade, it was around eighty million. Meanwhile, *The Jazz Singer* had introduced sound to the movies, and by 1930 color movies had taken the place of black-and-white.

# THE RADIO AGE

Alongside the automobile, the invention that most changed the lives of Americans in the 1920s was the radio. It was affordable even for ordinary families, so by 1928 some fifty million Americans listened on nine million radio sets to reports of Herbert Hoover's presidential victory. The devices linked rural communities to the wider world as never before. Between 1923 and 1930, 60 percent of American families owned one.

▼ A dairy farmer tunes his radio as he prepares to listen to a broadcast on headphones in the milking shed in 1923.

◀ *Harold Shaver of Jersey City takes a drawing lesson by radio; radio's ability to communicate seemed limitless.*

## AN EVENING IN

This was the schedule for Station WJZ, Newark, New Jersey, on October 12, 1922:
- 7:00 P.M.—"Jack Rabbit Stories," by David Cory.
- 8:30 P.M.—Closing prices on stocks, bonds, grain, coffee, and sugar.
- 8:36 P.M.—"Economizing Space with the Proper Wardrobe and Closets for Men's Clothes," by *Vanity Fair*.
- 8:40 P.M.—Concert by the Schubert Quartette.
- 9:30 P.M.—"The Merchant of Venice," a dramatic reading by Mona Morgan.
- 9:55 P.M.— Arlington Time Signals: Official Weather Forecast.

## SOURCE EXPLORED

This photograph from 1924 shows a young boy sketching a snowman as he listens to a drawing lesson on the radio. A wide range of shows were broadcast: news, sports, entertainment, religious sermons, and music. Evenings in millions of homes meant gathering around the radio to listen to music or stories. Radio stations sprang up across the country, paid for by commercials on behalf of advertisers who saw radio's potential to reach wide audiences. Radio was credited with helping Calvin Coolidge win the 1924 election after he made the first presidential radio broadcast on December 6, 1923. Coolidge's regular broadcasts made him familiar to the millions of Americans who voted for him as president.

# SPECULATION

▲ *Traders buy and sell shares in wheat on the floor of the Chicago Wheat Exchange early in the decade.*

As the 1920s progressed, many Americans had never had it so good. As well as the new automobile parked outside their home, they had many labor-saving devices inside. But these purchases were often bought on credit, and now storm clouds were gathering: auto sales were falling, as were the sales of many other consumer goods. Stores and warehouses were full, but factories kept producing goods. By 1929, a recession was imminent.

◄ Dozens of cars—mainly Fords—fill the parking lot of the new casino that opened in Miami Beach in 1923.

## SOURCE EXPLORED

Automobiles fill the parking lot of the new Miami Beach Casino in this photograph from 1923. Florida was promoted as a tropical paradise, and a real-estate boom began as investors were lured to buy land in Miami and the Everglades. Huge profits could be made by buying and selling land that the investor never even saw. The boom was short-lived. Much of the land proved to be useless swamp, and in 1926 a hurricane hit Miami. The city's image as a glamorous destination was destroyed—along with the savings of hundreds of thousands of small investors.

## AS THEY SAW IT

" From everywhere came the land-seekers, the profit-seekers. Automobiles moved along the Dixie Highway ... The license plates were from eighteen different states ... Most of the cars brimmed over with mother, father, grandmother, several children, and the dog, enticed by years of publicity about the miracles of Florida land values. "

—Gertrude Mathews Shelby on the Florida Land Boom, *Harper's Monthly*, January 1926

# THE WALL STREET CRASH

The stock market weakened in October 1929. On "Black Monday," October 28, panicking investors flooded the market with shares. As the cost of shares fell, many companies saw their value slashed, while investors had their savings wiped out. Confidence in the economy evaporated. Consumers stopped buying the goods that had fueled the boom of the 1920s.

▼ *A worried crowd gathers in Wall Street. Even ordinary Americans were involved in buying and selling stocks—and now stood to lose all their investments.*

## SOURCE EXPLORED

This print, titled *Dies Irae*—Latin for "Day of Wrath"—captures the shock of the Wall Street stock market crash. Artist James Rosenberg conveys the sense of panic that gripped investors in October 1929. The banks lining Wall Street appear to be collapsing, people are jumping from buildings, and lightning streaks across the sky in an apocalyptic scene. "Dies Irae" is a sentence used in the Roman Catholic funeral mass, so its use as an image title suggests that the world really is coming to an end.

▲ *Rosenberg's* Dies Irae *(1929) captures the apocalyptic feeling that came with the crash.*

Eliott V. Bell was a financial writer for the *New York Times.* He describes the effect on the people who worked in Wall Street of "Black Thursday," the day of the first Stock Market crash on October 24, 1929.

❝ The ticker, hopelessly swamped, fell hours behind the actual trading and became completely meaningless. Far into the night, and often all night long, lights blazed in the windows of the tall office buildings where margin clerks and bookkeepers struggled with the desperate task of trying to clear one day's business before the next began. They fainted at their desks; the weary runners fell exhausted on the marble floors of the banks and slept. But within a few months they were to have ample time to rest up. By then thousands of them had been fired. ❞

# THE DEPRESSION BEGINS

Nothing prepared Americans for the Great Depression. Following the Wall Street Crash of 1929, people nervous about their jobs stopped buying goods. Meanwhile, new tariffs designed to protect U.S. manufacturers from imports slowed down international trade. President Herbert Hoover hoped the situation would right itself. Instead the country plunged into a full-scale depression, as people lost their jobs and often their homes. Rather unfairly, Hoover took much of the blame. The clusters of shacks where the unemployed took shelter were named Hoovervilles.

◀ This Texan family lost their farm and income as the Depression hit. They became migrant fruit pickers in California.

Paul Angle, from Springfield, Illinois, describes how the Depression destroyed the price a farmer could get for his corn, making his crop worthless:

> One day in 1933 I met a friend in a bank in Springfield, Illinois, in the center of the corn belt. He was a hog buyer, much concerned with farm prosperity, much depressed by prevailing prices. During our conversation he took a fifty-cent piece from his pocket and threw it on one of the bank's gloss-topped writing tables. 'Paul Angle,' he exclaimed, 'You're a sturdy fellow, but you can't carry out of this bank all the corn that half-dollar will buy!' He was right: there are fifty-six pounds in a bushel of corn, and the price was then ten cents a bushel.

▲ New Yorkers wait in line for food beneath the Brooklyn Bridge. By 1932 nearly 25 percent of Americans were out of work and facing hardship.

### SOURCE EXPLORED

This photograph from the early 1930s shows a breadline beneath the Brooklyn Bridge in New York City. Lines of the poor waiting for handouts of food or for the chance of a hot meal became common in many cities as unemployment rose to between 25 and 35 percent of the workforce by early 1933. In Chicago, the notorious gangster Al Capone opened a soup kitchen to feed the poor.

# THE BONUS ARMY

▲ This photograph shows part of the shanty camp built by the veterans on Anacostia Flats on the edge of Washington, D.C.

**As the Depression took hold, President Hoover seemed incapable of reacting. His reputation fell further when around seventeen thousand World War I veterans and their supporters marched on Washington, D.C. in July 1932 to demand the early payment of war bonuses. Hoover sent in the Army to destroy the veterans' camp. The sight of their shelters burning profoundly upset many Americans and further damaged Hoover's reputation.**

◀ Veterans await the result of a congressional vote on paying their bonuses—the vote went against them, and they were told to disperse.

## THE BONUS

The bonus was intended to cover the difference between a soldier's pay and what he would have earned if he had stayed home. By 1932, however, the U.S. government could not afford to pay the bonus that had been promised in 1924—but which was not actually due to be paid until 1945.

Lee McCardell of the *Baltimore Sun* reports on General Douglas MacArthur's assault on the veterans' camp on July 29, 1932. Two babies died in the attack.

" The bonus army was retreating today—in all directions. Its billets destroyed, its commissary wrecked, its wives and babies misplaced, its leaders lost in the confusion which followed its rout last night by troops of the Regular Army, the former soldiers tramped the streets of Washington and the roads of Marylebone and Virginia, foraging for coffee and cigarettes ... The battle really had ended shortly after midnight ... The air was still sharply tainted with tear gas ... All Washington smelled a fight, and all Washington turned out to see it. Streets were jammed with automobiles. Sidewalks, windows, doorsteps were crowded with people trying to see what was happening. "

# THE ELECTION OF FDR

Franklin D. Roosevelt was in many ways an unlikely savior for struggling Americans. He came from an aristocratic family and had enjoyed a privileged upbringing before entering politics as a Democrat. When he ran against President Hoover in 1932, he promised to take positive steps to end the Depression. Roosevelt was so popular he was elected for four terms—but he was also divisive. Some Americans refused even to use his name, calling him only "That Man in the White House."

◀ Roosevelt (right) rides to his inauguration with his predecessor, Herbert Hoover, who was often blamed for not doing more to combat the effects of the Depression.

◀ *Franklin D. Roosevelt faces the microphones for a "fireside chat" about the drought afflicting the Midwest.*

## SOURCE EXPLORED

Franklin D. Roosevelt sits in front of radio microphones as he prepares to broadcast to Americans on September 6, 1936. Between 1933 and 1944, Roosevelt made thirty of his celebrated "fireside chats." Although radio had been around during the presidencies of Roosevelt's predecessors—Harding, Coolidge, and Hoover—none used radio as effectively as Roosevelt did. He understood that radio gave him the ability to connect directly with families in their own homes. The evening broadcasts were intended to explain specific measures—this one addressed a serious drought—and to reassure people that Roosevelt was dealing with the Depression. Roosevelt's friendly voice and informal way of speaking helped him broadcast to up sixty million people.

## AS THEY SAW IT

66 This is ... the time to speak the truth, the whole truth, frankly and boldly. Nor need we shrink from honestly facing conditions in our country today. This great Nation will endure as it has endured, will revive and will prosper. So, first of all, let me assert my firm belief that the only thing we have to fear is fear itself. 99

–FDR addresses Americans on his Inauguration Day, March 4, 1933

# THE NEW DEAL

Roosevelt took office on March 4, 1933, and that same day declared a four-day banking holiday to prevent bank failures. To pass legislation quickly, Roosevelt ordered a special session of Congress to approve measures to help struggling farmers and encourage employment. The new laws set up the "alphabet agencies," which were often known by their initials, such as the WPA (Works Progress Administration). In just 100 days, Congress passed all the major laws for what Roosevelt claimed was a "New Deal" for America.

SEE AMERICA
UNITED STATES TRAVEL BUREAU

◀ This poster was painted by Frank S. Nicholson in the late 1930s for a WPA campaign to promote tourism.

WORK PROMOTES CONFIDENCE

WORKS PROGRESS ADMINISTRATION

◀ *The Federal Art Project (FPA) produced this stylized poster encouraging workers to find confidence through their work.*

## AS THEY SAW IT

❝ I went to the poll line and voted
And I know I voted the right way
So I'm askin' you, Mr. President
Don't take away the W P and A. ❞

—Popular song about the **WPA** when Roosevelt was standing for reelection in 1936

## SOURCE EXPLORED

This poster, showing a stylized worker with a hammer, promoted the Works Progress Administration (WPA). Of all the many New Deal programs, the WPA affected most Americans. Before the program was canceled in 1943, it employed more than 8.5 million people and spent more than $11 million employing people on public works, building bridges, roads, public parks, and more than one thousand airports. In return workers earned an average salary of $41.57 a month. WPA director Harry Hopkins believed it was better for people's confidence and morale to pay them to work rather than give them unemployment benefit: "Give a man a dole, and you save his body and destroy his spirit. Give him a job and you save both body and spirit."

# LOOKING FOR WORK

As the Great Depression took hold, a drought gripped much of the agricultural heartland of the Midwest. As the drought worsened, people moved from the countryside. By 1935, more than a million people had quit the Plains to look for work in the cities; another 2.5 million left between 1935 and 1940. Around a million people headed west to California.

Meanwhile, men across the country were leaving their families and going anywhere there might be work. They often traveled by jumping on freight cars on the railroads.

▶ Men seeking work crowd outside an employment agency on Sixth Avenue in New York in December 1935.

## SOURCE EXPLORED

A man is helped to hop a freight car in Bakersfield, California, in April 1940. Hopping freight trains was popular because it was free—but it was also illegal. Up to two million men and eight thousand women traveled on the trains. They were known as "hoboes." The railroads hired guards to make sure that only paying travelers used the trains, so hoboes often ran alongside moving freight trains and jumped into open boxcars. It was a dangerous way to travel. In just one year, 6,500 hobos were killed by falling from trains or by being beaten by guards.

▲ *A man pulls a colleague into a boxcar. Jumping freight trains was highly dangerous and accidents were common.*

## AS THEY SAW IT

" In 1930 and 1931, you'd see freight trains, you'd see hundreds of kids, young kids, lots of 'em, just wandering all over the country ... Women gettin' places by ridin' freight trains. Dressed in slacks or dressed like men, you could hardly tell 'em ... "

—Jim Morrison,
Coal Miner in Indiana

# THE DUST BOWL

For much of the 1920s, farmers had overgrazed and overplowed the Great Plains. In the 1930s, high temperatures and windy conditions turned the fields into a vast dust bowl covering some 120,000 square miles (310,800 sq. km). Dry soil was whipped up and blown away. Clouds of dust up to 10,000 feet (3,000 m) high swept across the land. The dust filled peoples' lungs and jammed car engines.

No crops grew.

▼ *A farmer and his sons walk through a dust storm across land already covered with dust in Cimarron County, Oklahoma, 1936.*

## SOURCE EXPLORED

*Migrant Mother* is one of the most famous photographs of the Great Depression. It was taken in February or March 1936. The photographer, Dorothea Lange, worked for the Farm Security Administration (FSA) a government agency whose tasks included chronicling the effects of the Depression. The photograph shows Florence Thompson, a thirty-two-year-old migrant mother of seven, in a tent in Nipomo, California. Known as Okies, most of the migrant families came from the area worst hit by the dust storms—Oklahoma, Texas, Kansas, Colorado, and New Mexico.

▲ Migrant Mother *is one of a series of six images Dorothea Lange took of a destitute family in Nipomo, California.*

## AS THEY SAW IT

" I did not ask her name or her history. She told me her age, that she was thirty-two. She said that they had been living on frozen vegetables from the surrounding fields, and birds that the children killed. She had just sold the tires from her car to buy food. There she sat in that lean-to tent with her children huddled around her. "

—Dorothea Lange describes taking the photograph *Migrant Mother*

# THE CIVILIAN CONSERVATION CORPS

Roosevelt created the Civilian Conservation Corps in March 1933 to provide jobs for men between eighteen and twenty-five years of age. By June, more than 80,000 men were in 400 camps working on conservation schemes; another 155,000 were being trained. Some three million men joined the program over the next decade: they planted around 2.3 billion trees.

▲ Members of the CCC work in a Maryland forest in 1935. The outdoor work was designed to benefit not just the countryside but also the volunteers.

◀ *This poster was created in Illinois in 1941 to encourage young men to join the CCC.*

## AS THEY SAW IT

" These big trees you see along the highways—all these big forests was all built by the CCC. We went along plain barren ground. There were no trees. We just dug trenches and kept planting trees. You could plant about a hundred an hour. I really enjoyed it. I had three wonderful square meals a day. No matter what they put on the table, we ate, and were glad to get it. "

—Blackie Gold, a former car dealer, describes working for the CCC

## SOURCE EXPLORED

The face of the worker is blank apart from a broad smile. Perhaps this makes it easier for potential recruits to imagine themselves in his place. In its simple shapes and limited range of flat colors, it uses techniques developed by graphic artists in the Soviet Union in the early 1920s. There are other echoes of Soviet propaganda in the lettering, the CCC logo, and the heroic pose of the figure, who resembles an athlete. The CCC crest in the bottom corner confirms that the poster is an official document. At a time when not all Americans had radios, posters were a key way of communicating government messages to the population. Leading artists were commissioned to produce them.

## TIMELINE

| | |
|---|---|
| **1919** | ***January:*** *Congress ratifies the Eighteenth Amendment, prohibiting the manufacture or sale of alcohol.* |
| | ***June:*** *The Treaty of Versailles is signed in Paris; it imposes harsh fines on Germany for starting World War I, and creates the League of Nations to settle international disputes peacefully.* |
| **1920** | *The U.S. Senate refuses to ratify the Treaty of Versailles or join the League of Nations.* |
| | ***August 18:*** *Congress ratifies the Nineteenth Amendment, giving women the right to vote.* |
| | ***November 2:*** *Republican Warren G. Harding wins the presidential election by a landslide, promising a return to "normalcy."* |
| **1921** | ***May:*** *Congress imposes quotas on immigration from southern and eastern Europe.* |
| **1923** | ***April:*** *Yankee Stadium is built in the Bronx, New York.* |
| | ***August 23:*** *After President Harding dies of a stroke, Vice President Calvin Coolidge becomes president.* |
| **1925** | ***April:*** *F. Scott Fitzgerald publishes* The Great Gatsby. |
| | *The Charleston becomes a popular dance craze; the women who dance it are called Flappers.* |
| | ***August 8:*** *Forty thousand members of the Ku Klux Klan march in Washington, D.C.* |
| **1927** | ***May 21:*** *Charles Lindbergh completes the first solo flight across the Atlantic in his airplane, the* Spirit of St. Louis. |
| | ***October 6:*** *The Jazz Singer, with Al Jolson, becomes the first talking picture.* |
| **1928** | ***November 6:*** *Republican Herbert Hoover wins the presidential election.* |
| **1929** | ***February 14:*** *In Chicago, Al Capone's gang murder six members of a rival gang in the Saint Valentine's Day Massacre.* |
| | ***October:*** *The stock market in Wall Street crashes, signaling the start of the Great Depression.* |
| **1930** | *The Smoot-Hawley Tariff is introduced to protect U.S. businesses; it greatly slows down global trade, helping the Depression to spread.* |

**1931**    Unemployment averages 16.3 percent.

**May 1:** In New York City, the Empire State Building becomes the tallest building in the world.

**December:** The Bank of the United States in New York collapses.

**1932**    Unemployment averages 24.1 percent.

Democrat Franklin D. Roosevelt defeats Herbert Hoover in the presidential election by a landslide.

**1933**    **March 4:** Roosevelt takes office, and begins a rapid program of legislation to lay the foundations of what he calls the "New Deal," a series of measures to get Americans back to work.

The Twenty-First Amendment repeals Prohibition.

Adolf Hitler, leader of the National Socialist, or Nazi, Party, becomes chancellor of Germany.

**1934**    Drought turns large areas of the Midwest into a Dust Bowl.

Unemployment averages 21.7 percent.

**1935**    Unemployment averages 20.1 percent.

**April:** The Works Progress Administration is created to help the economy by employing millions of Americans on public works.

**1936**    Roosevelt is elected for a second term, again by a landslide. The Hoover Dam, one of the great public works of the Depression, opens on the border of Arizona and Nevada.

**1937**    Unemployment averages 14.3 percent.

**1938**    European leaders are powerless to halt Hitler's demands for more territory in Europe; the Nazi Party begins to dismantle democracy in Germany.

**1939**    John Steinbeck publishes The Grapes of Wrath, his novel about "Oakies" migrating to California.

**September 1:** Germany invades Poland, leading Britain and France to declare war. World War II in Europe has begun.

# GLOSSARY

**apocalyptic** Related to the complete destruction of the world.

**boom** A period when economic activity increases very rapidly.

**consumerism** The aquisition of increasing numbers of goods and services.

**credit** A system by which a customer can obtain goods or services but pay for them in the future.

**depression** A long and severe slowdown in a country's economy.

**dole** A gift of food, money, or clothing given to the poor.

**drought** A period of unusually low rainfall that leads to water shortages.

**hobo** A homeless migrant worker.

**isolationism** A policy of avoiding involvement in the political affairs of other countries.

**migrant** A person who moves from one place to another in order to find work or better living conditions.

**nostrum** A remedy proposed for curing a social problem.

**pandemic** Something that affects many individuals, a whole country, or the whole world, such as an outbreak of disease.

**prohibition** The prevention by law of the manufacture and sale of alcohol, as applied in the United States from 1920 to 1933.

**public works** Large construction schemes such as bridges or schools, carried out by the government for the benefit of the community.

**ratify** To officially approve an agreement or treaty.

**recession** A period of at least six months when a country's trade and industrial activity are in decline.

**shares** Units that entitle their holders to a share of the capital value of a company; shares are widely traded, and their value goes up and down.

**soup kitchen** A place where free food is provided for the poor or homeless.

**speakeasy** An establishment that illegally sold liquor during Prohibition.

**stock market** A place where people trade in shares.

**tariff** A tax or duty paid on a particular type of import or export.

**ticker** A machine that prints out stock-market information on a strip of paper.

## FURTHER INFORMATION

# Books

Corrigan, Jim. *The 1920s: The Roaring Twenties.* Amazing Decades in Photos. Berkeley Heights, NJ: Enslow Publishers Ltd, 2010.

Gitlin, Martin. *The Prohibition Era.* Essential Events. Minneapolis, MN: Abdo Publishing Company, 2010.

Hakim, Joy. *War, Peace, and All That Jazz: 1918–1945.* A History of US. New York: Oxford University Press, 2007.

Johnson, Robin. *The Great Depression.* Crabtree Chrome. Mankato, MN: Crabtree Publishing Company, 2014.

Maupin, Melissa. *Franklin D. Roosevelt.* Presidents of the USA. Mankato, MN: The Child's World, Inc, 2014.

McNeese, Tim. *World War I and the Roaring Twenties 1914–1928.* Discovering U.S. History. New York: Chelsea House Publishers, 2010.

Price, Sean. *America Has Fun: The Roaring Twenties.* American History Through Primary Sources. North Mankato, MN: Raintree Fusion, 2008.

# Websites

**www.gilderlehrman.org/history-by-era/progressive-era-new-era-1900-1929/roaring-twenties**
Essay from the Gilder Lehrman Institute of American History with links to primary sources.

**www.pbs.org/wgbh/americanexperience/films/dustbowl**
Film on the Dust Bowl from the PBS series *The American Experience*.

**www.u-s-history.com/pages/h1564.html**
United States History.com summary of the Roaring Twenties, with many links.

**Publisher's note to educators and parents:** Our editors have carefully reviewed these websites to ensure that they are suitable for students. Many websites change frequently, however, and we cannot guarantee that a site's future contents will continue to meet our high standards of quality and educational value. Be advised that students should be closely supervised whenever they access the Internet.

# INDEX